WHO LIVES AT THE SEASHORE?

Animal Life Along the Shore

GLENN O. BLOUGH

PICTURES BY
JEANNE BENDICK

Purple House Press
Kentucky

WALKING ALONG THE SEASHORE

If you walk along the seashore on a bright summer day, you will feel the sun warm on your head and feel the tingle of sea spray cool on your cheeks, but all around nothing may seem to move except the water that is lapping at your feet. Then, suddenly, a bird calls, and you look up at the blue sky to see gulls sailing overhead. As you watch, they may flap their wings and dive toward the sea, and you may think, "Gulls live by the shore but I don't see anything else."

Some strange and wonderful things happen along the seashore. But many of the creatures are hard to see unless you know where to look.

If you look down at the sand you may see a starfish or two in a pool. They are often washed upon the shore. You may think, "Gulls and starfish live by the shore, but that's about all."

If you dig down in the sand in the right place you may find clams buried in the wet sand, and then you may say, "Gulls and starfish and clams live by the shore, but probably that's about all."

If you look closely at rocks and pieces of wood, you may find barnacles fastened to them and find some seaweed. Then you may say, "Gulls and starfish and clams and barnacles and seaweed live by the shore, but probably nothing more."

As you walk along where the tide comes and goes you may find shells of different kinds. Some are empty. Some have animals in them. By now you will know that many animals live on the shore where the water meets the sand and the sky is blue. But it takes quite a lot of looking to find these animals.

You may discover an animal that has no house of its own. It lives in the house of another animal. You may see an animal drop clam shells on rocks to break them open. You may even see an animal that pushes its stomach out of its mouth when it eats. It usually has five arms. If one gets broken off it can grow a new one.

Come along to the shore, where the water meets the sand, and let's see who lives there. Let's stop and listen. Hear the gulls and sandpipers? Let's take a deep breath. Smell the sun—clams—fish—seas, smell? Take off your shoes and socks. Feel the sand? Now let's look around.

High tide

WATCHING THE TIDES

All day long and all night long the tide comes and goes at the seashore. When the tide is coming in, the water begins to cover the sand and the stones and everything else that is near the edge of the sea. The water keeps coming in and coming in and getting higher and higher on the shore. When the water stops getting higher we say that it is high tide.

When the tide is on its way out, the water keeps going out and going out and getting lower and lower on the shore. The sand, the stones, and everything near the edge of the sea where the water has been look dark and damp, but you can walk on them now. When the tide stops getting lower we say that it is low tide.

Low tide

In every twenty-four-hour day there is a low tide, followed by a high tide, and then a second low tide, followed by a second high tide. High tide, low tide, high tide, low tide—that's the way it is every day.

The tide makes a big difference to animals and plants that live along the shore. When the tide is in, many shore animals like clams and snails are under the water. When the tide is out, animals like horseshoe crabs are lying on the land. Some animals come in with the tide when it comes in, and then they go out when the tide goes out. Jellyfish do, and so do other animals. But often they get left on the land when the tide goes out. Sometimes they are caught in little pools of water and sometimes they are left on land. This happens to starfish and hermit crabs too. This is one thing that makes a walk along the seashore exciting, especially when the tide goes out.

Some animals and plants live far back from the shore. They get wet only when the high tide is very, very high. Clams and mussels live just at the edge of the sea or just in it. They are almost always wet except when the low tide is very, very low. Many animals live in between these two places. They get wet, then they get dry, then they get wet again, and they get dry again.

The water of the seashore is smooth and quiet when the weather is pleasant. The water laps against the sandy shore as if the sea and shore like each other. But the sea becomes rough before a storm and sometimes giant waves come rolling to the shore. The whitecaps come crashing against the shore one after the other. Some of the animals that live in the water are thrown to the beach. Even some of the animals that live on the bottom of the sea are tossed to the land. You may see these animals if you walk along the shore after a storm.

There are many different kinds of seashores around the United States. Some are rocky. Waves dash against these rocky shore when the weather is stormy. When the tide is out, many of the rocks are on dry land. When the tide is in, some of them are under the water. Many kinds of animals and plants live on these rocks or between them or under them.

Some seashores on the open ocean are smooth and sandy and the water is fine for swimming. Sometimes the seashore curves in and out and makes bays and coves where the water is quiet. Many kinds of animals may be found when the tide comes and goes in these quiet waters. Often these shores are muddy, and clams and other animals can be found there. Some seashore animals like rocky beaches, some like sandy beaches, and others like mud.

Come for a walk along the shore where tides come and go and waves roll in, and see what you can see. This is no time to skip. You won't see much if you do. You will see more if you walk. You will see more if you take along a magnifying glass. Look once. Then look again with your magnifying glass and you will see twice as much or even more.

If you go to the seashore, especially in the summer, you can make many discoveries. But you must learn *when* to look and *how* to look and *where* to look. Then you will see for yourself some of the things that you will read about between here and the end of the book.

DIGGING FOR CLAMS

If you are on a seashore where the mud is soft and sandy and the tide is low, look for clams. You can tell where they are sometimes by the holes in the sand. But if you disturb them, sometimes they squirt water up out of the sand.

Some clams are fast diggers. Razor clams cut deeply into the moist sand so fast that you must dig quickly or you will not find them. A razor clam is long and narrow and very good to eat. Many people call these clams, cutters, because they go so fast.

Razor clam

There are many other kinds of clams that live at the seashore. They are different shapes and sizes and they are found living on many different seashores around the Unites States.

Hard-shell clams have thick, hard shells

Soft-shell clams have thin, brittle shells

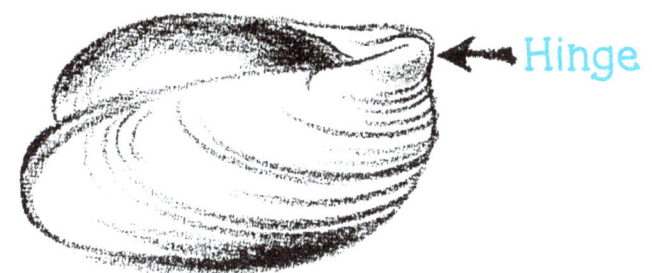

Look at the pictures here and you will see that a clam shell is made of two parts that fold together like the covers of a book. The clam opens up like a book, and the clam's soft body is inside. See the hinge on one side of the clam shell? Very strong muscles hold the two shell parts together.

Clams almost always stay in the sand or mud. Some stay near the top of the sand and some dig down. The clam's body usually has two tubes that stick out between the shells when they open. If the clam is in the water you can see these tubes. If it is buried under the sand or mud, the tubes come up to the top. The clam draws water through one of these tubes and releases it through the other tube. The water that is drawn into the clam carries the food inside. When the water is taken in so are tiny water animals and plants and small eggs of other animals, and the clam eats them.

A hard-shell clam

A soft-shell clam

It is hard to tell how a clam eats just by watching it. You can't watch its mouth open and shut because its mouth is inside the shell.

Did you ever see a clam walking? A clam has only one foot and it really doesn't look like the kind of foot most animals have. It is the part of the clam that sticks out between its two shells. When the clam walks, it pushes this foot out into the sand. The end of the foot holds onto the sand, and then the clam pulls the rest of itself up to the end of the foot. Then it pushes its foot out again, and so on and on. This may seem like a slow way to walk, but some clams are faster then you can imagine.

A clam's tube is called a siphon   Foot

The clam grows its own shell and the shell becomes larger as the clam grows. The animal uses lime from the water to build its hard shell. Clam shells are easy to find on many seashores. There are hard-shell clams and calico clams and little-neck clams and pismo clams—and more, too.

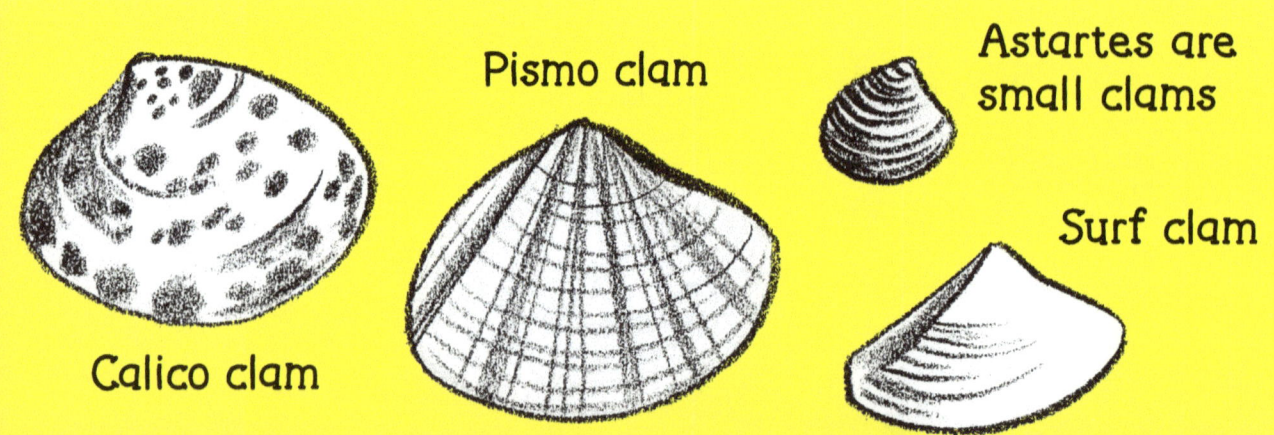

Calico clam

Pismo clam

Astartes are small clams

Surf clam

Probably you think that a clam is perfectly safe inside its shell with strong muscles to hold it shut. But you are mistaken. Hundreds of tiny clams are eaten by big fish and all sorts of other hungry water animals. But even after clams are larger and their shells are hard, they are still not safe from danger.

Gulls eat clams. Of course, they don't care for the hard shells, but they do like the soft body inside. Can you guess how they get the body inside? Do you think they catch them when their shells are open? Even gulls are not quick enough for this. Do you suppose that they open them with their beaks? No! Maybe they open them with their feet? No!

Gulls have a very interesting way of opening clam shells. The gulls find the clams on the beach and take them in their beaks, and away they fly over a pile of rocks on the seashore. Then they drop the clams on the hard rocks. This breaks the shell, and the gull flies down and eats its lunch. If the shell doesn't break the first time it is dropped, the gull picks it up and drops it again.

Some sea snails eat clams too. The kind of snail that you have in your aquarium couldn't eat a clam, but many kinds of sea snails can. These snails have a tongue that's like a drill. They climb on the shell of a clam and begin to drill. They drill and drill until finally they get through the hard shell. Then they stick a tube through this hole and eat the soft body inside. You may find clam shells with holes drilled in them. When you find a shell like this you will know what has happened.

There is still another animal that can eat clams and you wouldn't think it could. It has no drill, but that doesn't keep it from eating clams and oysters. You will see a picture of this animal eating a clam later in this book.

Oysters are cousins of clams. They have two shells and eat in the same way that clams do. Oysters have some of the same troubles that clams have. A snail called the oyster drill eats oysters, and so does that other animal which you will learn about later.

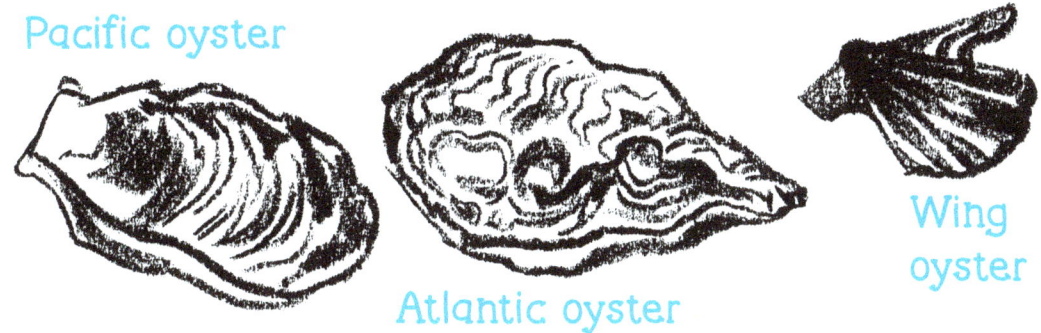

Pacific oyster
Atlantic oyster
Wing oyster

Mussels are clams' cousins too. You often find bunches of them washed up on the shore or fastened to pieces of wood in the water. There are blue mussels and hooked mussels and several other kinds.

Mussels make threads that hold them to rocks or boards or to each other. That's why you often find them in bunches.

Mussel shells are easy to find on nearly every ocean beach, and so are the shells of other water animals. Let's look for them.

Blue mussel

Hooked mussel

LOOKING FOR SHELLS

If you look carefully and in the right places you will find many kinds of shells on the seashore. They are different colors. Some are brightly colored—as yellow as the sun or as blue as the sky. Some are the color of sand and mud.

Shells are found in many sizes. Some are so small that they are hard to see. Others are large and therefore easy to find. Shells are different shapes. Some are shaped like ice cream cones, some are round, some are shaped like jack knives, and some look like small slippers. Clam shells are made of two parts, but snail shells have only one part.

Coquinas Sand dollars Cowries Scallops

Shells on the beach are different colors, sizes, and shapes, but they are all alike in one way. They are all parts of animals. They empty shells you find on the beach are what is left over after the animal inside has died.

You might like to make a collection of seashell animals. You could have many different kinds of shells in it—bright ones, dull ones, small ones, large ones, round ones, and cone-shaped ones. You might call it a "What's-Left-Over" collection, because so many of the things you will find to put in it are the parts of the sea animals that are left over after the animal dies.

On almost any seashore you might find these shells

Razor clams
Jingle shells
Moon shells
Mussels
Periwinkles
Cockles
Hornshells
Tellins

More shells on pages 24-25

A seashell is the outside cover of an animal. The animal grew this outside cover. At first the animal was small. So was the shell. But as the animal grew larger so did the shell. That is what happened to the clam.

Many of the shells you find on the beach are empty. The animals inside the shells have died. But you may find shells with the animal still inside. Sometimes you may pick up a shell and not know that there is an animal inside. It may have its door shut, and you won't know that the animal is at home.

Some of the shells on the shore are sea snail shells. Some of these look like the snails that you see in an aquarium. Many of them are much larger, and you wouldn't think they are snails at all.

Periwinkles are small

Look for periwinkles on seaweed or weed-covered rocks

One of the smallest kind of sea snails is called the periwinkle. There are different kinds of periwinkles, and they live on the rocks on beaches where the tide comes and goes. Sometimes they are underwater, but often they are on dry land. When the tide goes out and leaves them dry, the periwinkle pulls its body into its shell and closes its shell door. This keeps the soft body inside from drying out. If the body gets too dry the animal dies. When the tide comes in and the animal is wet, the door opens and the head and foot come out. The animals begins to creep around to find food and do other things that snails do when they are on the move.

A snail's foot is flat and wide. It is a very important part of the snail's body. The snail creeps from one place to another on it.

If you have watched a snail in an aquarium you know that it has a head with feelers on it. If it was eating on the side of the aquarium you may have seen its mouth. If you looked with a magnifying glass, you may have seen its tongue, which is very rough and just perfect for scraping off green scum and other food.

When a periwinkle stops growing it is hardly an inch long. Its tongue is much longer, and there are hundreds and hundreds of rough places on it that are like teeth. Such a tongue is handy for eating. Periwinkles eat sea plants.

You already know about a very remarkable thing that some sea snails can do with their rough tongues. They use them to drill holes in the shells of other animals like clams, and then they eat the soft inside parts.

One of the most interesting sea snails you will ever find on the seashore is the queen conch.

Queen conch

It lives on sandy sea bottoms where the water is not very deep. The conch is a much bigger snail than the ones in your aquarium and hardly looks anything like an aquarium snail. It has a foot with a special part which can reach into the sand and help the heavy snail jump. When a queen conch walks, it jumps and the big shell flaps from side to side. You would have fun watching a queen conch walk.

The conch uses its tongue to drill holes just as many of the other snails do.

Did anyone ever tell you that you can hear the sound of the sea if you listen to a conch shell? It may sound like the roar of the sea, but it is not. The sound you hear in a seashell is not from the sea, unless you are near the sea. It comes from the air in the shell and from all the sounds that are around you that reach your ear through the shell.

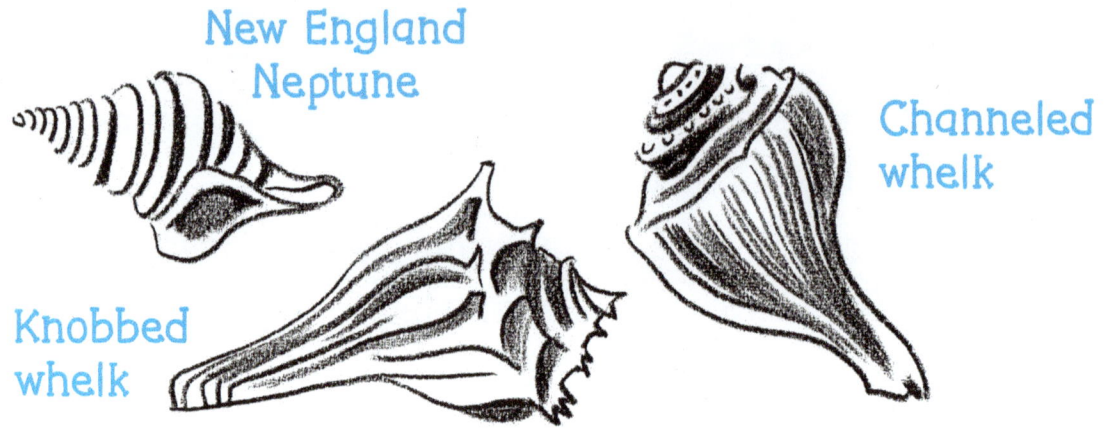

If you ever found a whelk shell you would be very excited. They are large like conch shells, and there are several kinds.

On one of your walks along the beach you may find something that looks like the picture on this page. Can you imagine what it is? It doesn't look like a shell, does it? It doesn't look like an animal either. And it is not a sea plant. Look at it very closely and you will see the tiny holes in each part of it. Use a magnifying glass and you can see them very easily. Shake the shell. Do you think there is anything inside?

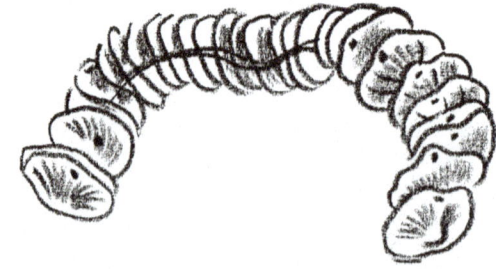

Hold a piece of paper under one of the holes to catch anything that might fall out. Some things will, and, if you look at them through the magnifying glass, you will see tiny objects like the ones you see under the magnifying glass on this page. They are many tiny, tiny shells that look exactly like the big whelk shell except they are much, much, much smaller. Now do you know what you have found?

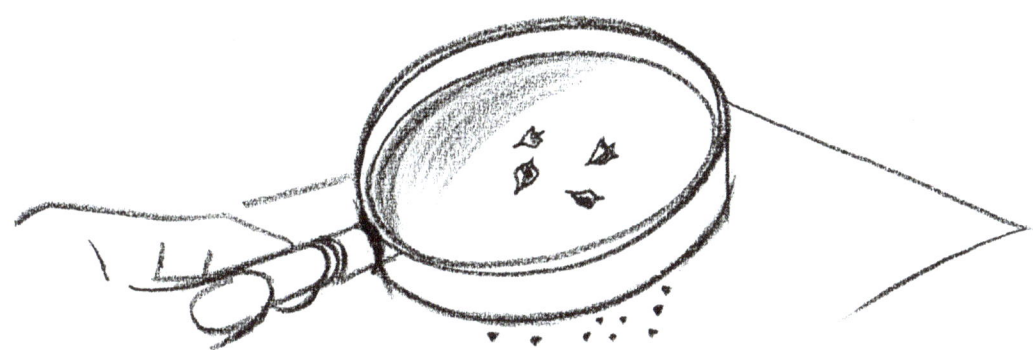

Whelks lay their eggs in these long chains of egg cases. The eggs are inside these cases. There are many eggs. Each one hatches into a tiny whelk. Each case has a tiny hole that lets the tiny new whelks out.

There are more kinds of shells on a seashore than you can tell about in one book. There are moon shells and volcanic shells and rock shells and cowrie shells and on and on. If you make a What's-Left-Over collection, shells will make up a big part of it. They will make your collection interesting and bright. The more you learn about the animals that lived in these leftovers, the more fun you will have with your collection.

SHELLS FOR YOUR

If you live on the Pacific Coast, you might find

Giant keyhole limpets

Abalones

Olives

Pismo clams

Scallops

Sand dollars

Frilled dogwinkles

Bubble shells

AND MORE

If you live on the South Atlantic Coast, you might find

Fig shells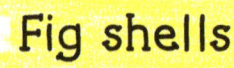

Augers

Conchs

Turkey wings

Murex shells

Lucinas

WHAT'S-LEFT-OVER COLLECTION

If you live on the North or Central Atlantic Coast, you might find

On the Gulf Coast you might find

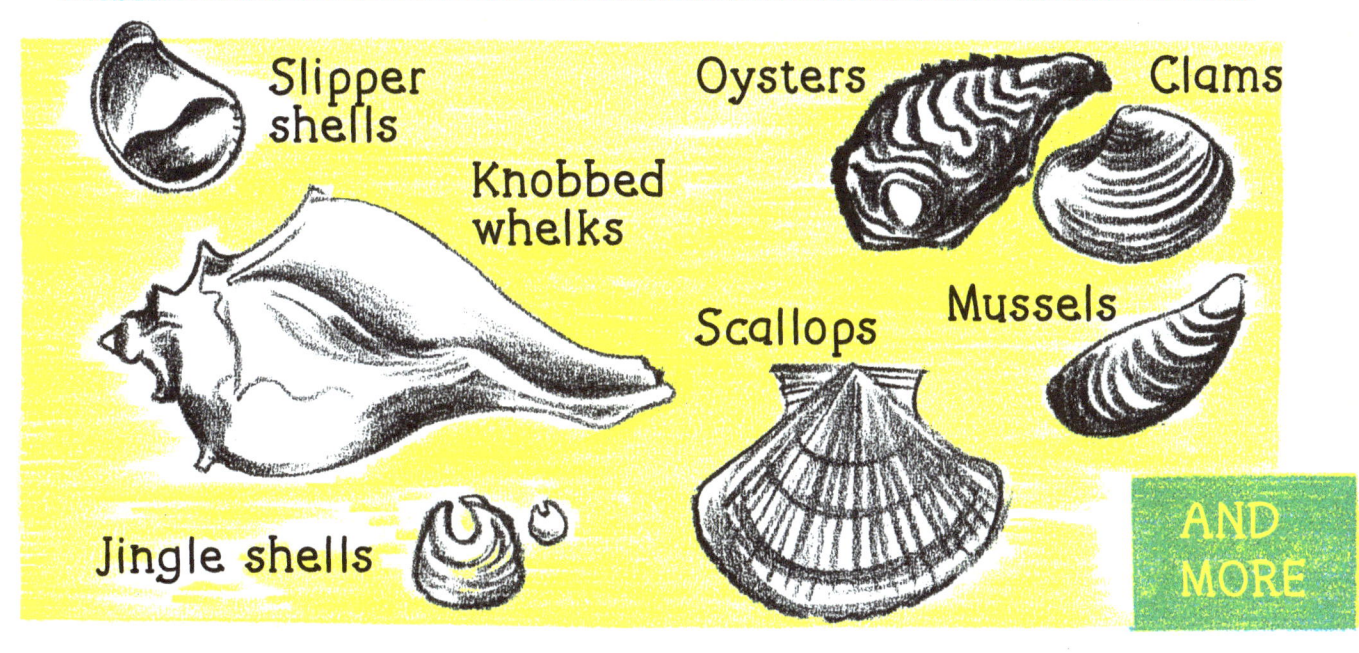

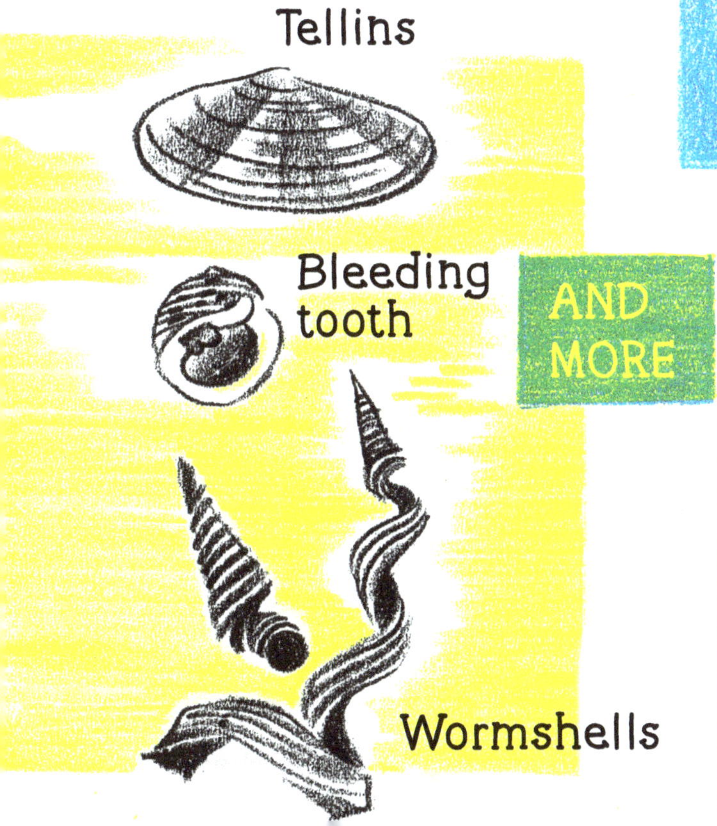

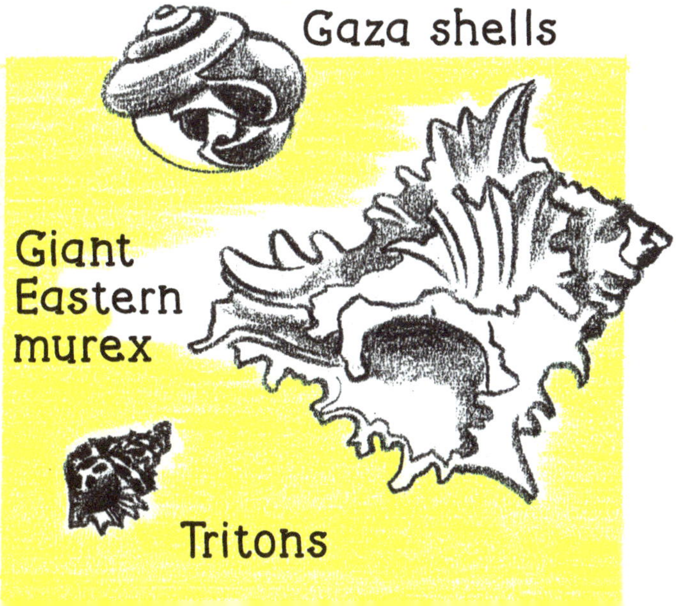

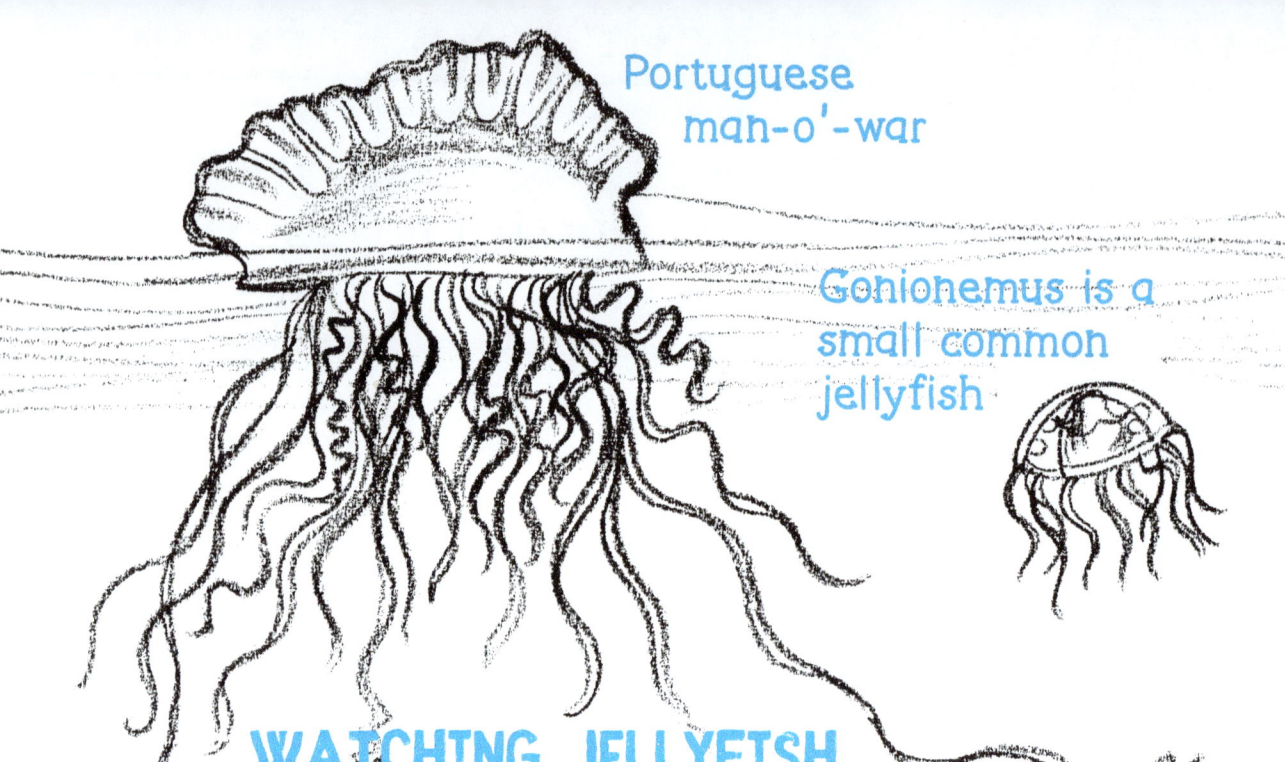

Portuguese man-o'-war

Gonionemus is a small common jellyfish

WATCHING JELLYFISH

On the sandy beach, when the tide is out, you may sometimes find a lump of jelly. It has no shape. It is just a pile of jelly. If it has been in the sun very long, the water in it has dried up and there is almost nothing left. A jellyfish is almost all water, and the skin on the outside is not very thick, so a jellyfish dries out very fast if it is not in the water.

A jellyfish is not a fish at all. It has no scales or fins as real fish do. It has no backbone as real fish do. It has no bones at all. That's why it has no shape when you find it on the beach. When a jellyfish is in the water it is shaped like an umbrella—but without much of a handle. You can see that water makes a lot of difference to a jellyfish.

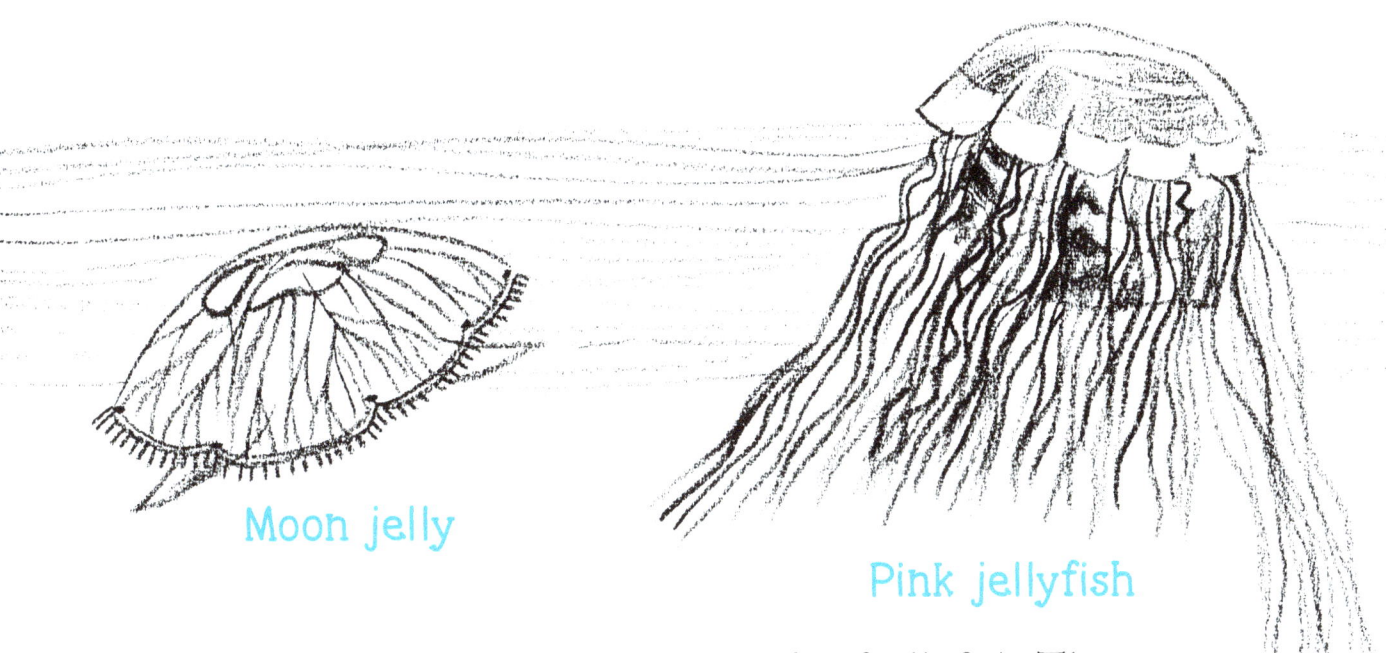

Moon jelly

Pink jellyfish

A moon jelly is one of the kinds of jellyfish. The moon jelly has a mouth. It has feelers and eyes. It has stingers and fringes. You can see some of these parts of a moon jelly if you find one floating in the water near the shore. You can't see the mouth because it's under the umbrella, but you can see the feelers, and the stingers are in these feelers. These stingers have poison in them. The dots on the edge of the umbrella are the moon jelly's eyes. They are not very good eyes. The moon jelly can't see very far or very well. Those parts that look like ribbons that hang down from the mouth help the jellyfish to catch food.

Real fish use their fins and tails to push through the water, but jellyfish just float along in the water and help themselves move by opening and closing their umbrellas.

Those stingers around the edge of the umbrella are for food-catching and for keeping enemies away. The stingers shoot out when something touches them. If it's something which is good food for a jellyfish, the ribbons that hang down guide the food into its mouth. If it's you that the jellyfish touches, you may be sorry because the poison in the stingers makes your skin itch and burn. It's a good thing to stay away from jellyfish washed up on the beach and from floating jellyfish when you are in swimming. This is one of the things you will soon find out if you are not careful.

Some jellyfish don't swim around. They grow on rocks or seaweed and look like plants.

Tubularia

Obelia

Some jellyfish, like moon jellies, glow at night. Some jellyfish are large. Some are small. Some are the color of the water, and some are pink or blue or orange.

You won't have any jellyfish in your What's-Left-Over collection. It's not hard to guess why, is it?

FINDING STARFISH

Storms sometimes toss starfish onto the sandy shore. Sometimes they ride in on the tide and are left on the shore when the tide goes out. You may find them in the tiny pools of water that are left on the shore when the tide goes out. You may find them on the rocks on the shore too.

A starfish is not a fish any more than a jellyfish is a fish. It doesn't look anything like a fish, for it has no scales or fins. Usually a starfish has five arms. If you look carefully at the ends of these arms you will see small dots. They are eyes. But they do not see well. About the best they can do is to tell if it is light or dark.

If you turn a starfish over you will see its mouth. The mouth is on the bottom side where the arms meet. The arms are covered with a very rough skin with spines on it. If you look closely at the bottom side of the starfish, you will see a long groove that goes from the mouth to the ends of each of the arms. There are tiny holes along these grooves, and the starfish has tiny tubes that can push out through these holes. They are called tube feet. There are hundreds of these tube feet. The starfish uses these tube feet for crawling over stones and wherever else it crawls. It uses them when it eats too.

A starfish is a funny eater. It is one of the enemies of clams and oysters. If you watched a starfish eat a clam, you would be very surprised. The starfish uses those tube feet on its arms. Each one of these tube feet is like a tiny suction cup and can pull on anything it touches. A starfish which is hungry for a clam dinner wraps its

arms around the clam and the tube feet fasten on the shells. Then the feet begin to pull on the clam shell to open it. They pull and pull. The clam holds its shell together as tightly as it can. The starfish pulls more. The clam tries not to let its shell open. The strong muscles hold it shut. The starfish pulls more and more and harder and harder. Finally the clam opens, and then something very surprising happens. The starfish pushes its own stomach out through its mouth into the clam shell and eats the soft parts inside.

Many people do not know this surprising thing about how a starfish eats. Many people have never seen it happen. But people who walk along beaches and watch closely and stand quietly have seen it happen.

There are many kinds of starfish

A starfish can do something that most animals cannot do. Dogs and cats can't do it. Birds can't do it, and neither can you. A starfish can grow new parts to its body. If something happens to an arm of a starfish it can grow a new one! A starfish can grow several new arms. If an enemy of the starfish catches its arm and bites it off it can grow a new one. If a starfish gets cut in two, each one of the parts can grow into a new starfish—which is a long task that can take up to a year to do.

Some oyster growers used to cut starfish apart and throw them back in the water. They thought that the starfish would die. But when they learned that starfish could grow new parts they stopped doing this. A starfish is interesting in a What's-Left-Over collection. When you add a starfish to your collection you have almost all of its body.

Starfish have interesting cousins. You wouldn't think these creatures were related to starfish. They are not shaped like starfish, but most of them do have spiny skin. One cousin is the sea urchin. Another is the sand dollar, and another is the sea cucumber. Some sea urchins live in shallow water and some live where it is deep. Some are purple colored. Some are green. Some have long, heavy spines.

Sea urchin

What's left over looks like this

Sand dollars are flatter than sea urchins and live in deep water. You often find them dead on the beach. You can't spend sand dollars, but their skeletons are beautiful to keep around the house and look at and to have in a What's-Left-Over collection.

Sand dollars

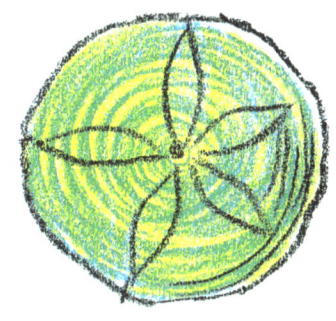

Sea cucumbers are long and spiny. Some are as long as fifteen or eighteen inches, and some are short. They are about the shape of a cucumber. You can find them under rocks on the seashore sometimes.

Sea cucumber

WATCHING CRABS

Hermit crabs are fun to find. Often you can find several of them in one pool. If you gather four or five and put them in a jar you may be surprised at what happens.

Hermit crabs don't make shells to live in as snails do. They live in what's left over from another animal. They find empty snail shells that fit them, and then they move in.

Snail shells are perfect homes for hermit crabs. The hermit crab backs into the shell and twists the back part of its body around and just fits into the shell. Its tail catches on to the tiniest twist way inside the shell, and you might think that the crab has grown into the shell because it fits so tightly. It hasn't though, and that is a good thing because the hermit crab keeps growing, and one day it will be too big for the shell it's living in. Then it's moving time for the hermit crab. It looks around for a bigger shell, and when it finds one it creeps out of the old shell and backs into the new one.

Out of the shell, this part is unprotected

Inside the shell is safety

Hermit crabs don't lose any time on moving day. While they are out of a shell they are not protected. They may be eaten by some other animal enemy, or another hermit crab may come along and eat them. When they are inside the shell they are very well protected. You will discover this if you very gently tug on the hermit crab. The crab moves way back into the snail shell and has folded together its front claws. The crab is in its house, out of danger. It's when the crab is out of the shell home and moving to a new one that it's in all kinds of danger from its enemies.

The front part of the crab has a hard covering to protect itself when it's sticking out of the shell. The tail parts are soft but they are protected by the shell that the animal lives in. No wonder the hermit crab doesn't stay out of the shell very long. Gulls and other animals along the shore eat hermit crabs.

If you watch the hermit crabs in your jar you may see them fight one another. They open their claws and pull at one another. They roll each other over. You might start out with four hermit crabs, later in the jar there may be only three. Sometimes the hermit crabs eat one other.

Hermit crabs are fun to watch in a tide pool. They are quite lively as they go about finding food. They travel faster than you think they can with their snail shell houses dragging along on top of them.

Fiddler crabs lives on seashores, too, but they are a little harder to find because they live in holes in the sand. The opening of a fiddler crab's under-the-sand home is usually on the beach just near the place where the tide comes when it's highest. Just before the tide gets highest the fiddler crab closes the door to its home so the tide doesn't come in and wash the animal away.

If you take more than one look at a fiddler crab and use your imagination a little, you will see how it gets its name. The male crab has one front claw which is much larger than the other. When he waves this large claw around in the air and holds up the smaller one at the same time, you can imagine that the big one is the fiddle and the small one is a bow. Maybe *you* wouldn't think so, but somebody did, and that's how the fiddler crab got its name.

Blue crab

Spider crab

Sand crabs are little

There are many other kinds of crabs that live in the water near the shore of the sea. There are blue crabs that are very good to eat, and there are spider crabs and many other kinds.

A horseshoe crab is a very interesting animal that is often found on the seashore. It does not look at all like other crabs for it does not belong to the crab family. It comes nearer to being in the spider family. Horseshoe crabs often get washed up on the beach, and if you turn them over you can see how they crawl. You will see the legs underneath. You often find horseshoe crabs in a What's-Left-Over collection.

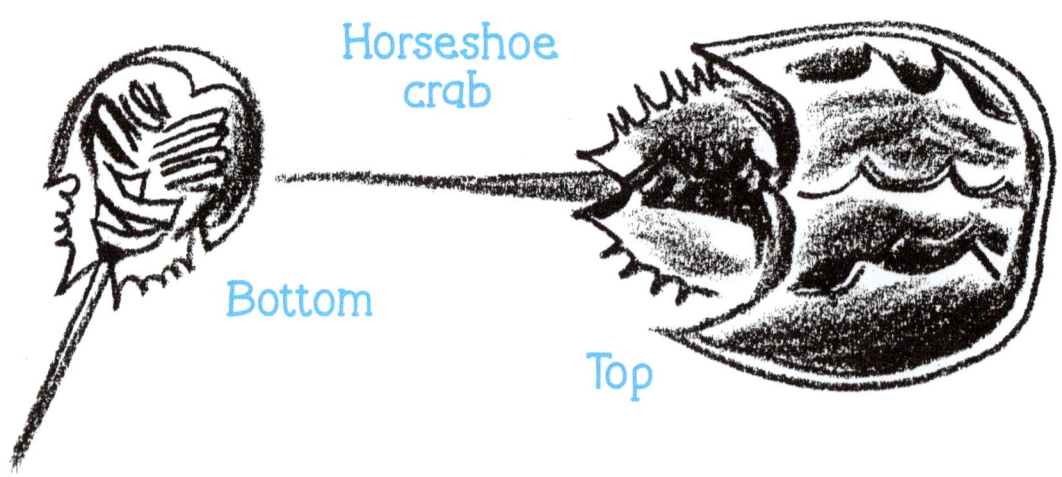

Horseshoe crab

Bottom

Top

Gooseneck barnacles

EXAMINING BARNACLES

Sometimes, on the beach you may find an old piece of driftwood which the sea has tossed up on the shore, and it may be covered with animals like the one in the picture here. They are gooseneck barnacles. They are the kind that sometimes grow on ships and are often found on pieces of floating wood.

If you look at rocks and posts that are sometimes underwater at high tide, you will probably see another kind of barnacle called rock barnacles. They often live where the tide comes and goes, and there may be thousands of them growing on one small rock or piece of wood.

Rock barnacles

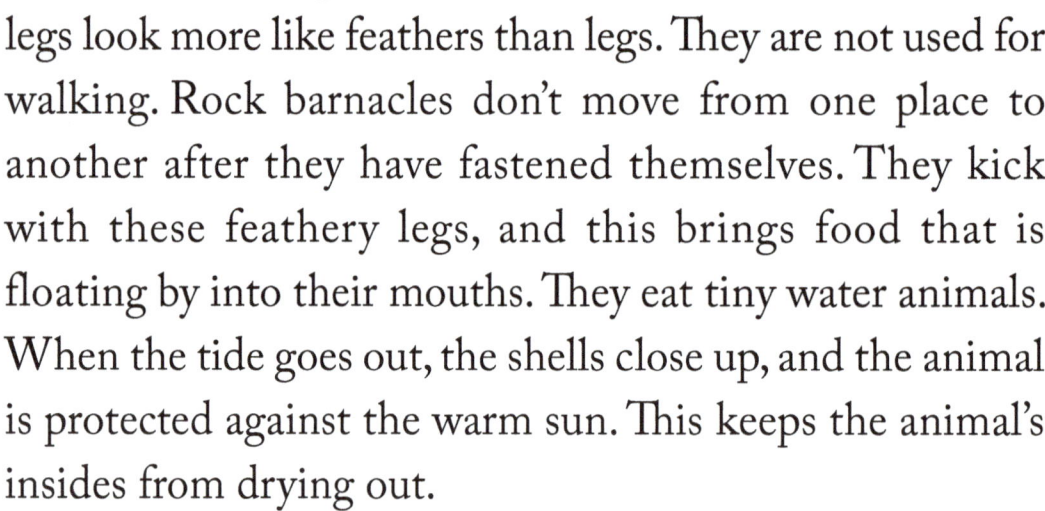

Rock barnacles have shells on their outsides. These shells can open and close. Rock barnacles change with the tides. When a barnacle is underwater its shell opens up and the barnacle's legs come out. Its legs look more like feathers than legs. They are not used for walking. Rock barnacles don't move from one place to another after they have fastened themselves. They kick with these feathery legs, and this brings food that is floating by into their mouths. They eat tiny water animals. When the tide goes out, the shells close up, and the animal is protected against the warm sun. This keeps the animal's insides from drying out.

It's fun to watch live barnacles. Find some underwater and put your face near enough to the water to get a good look. An even better way is to find a small stone with barnacles on it and put it in a dish of seawater and watch the barnacles with a magnifying glass, releasing the barnacles back to the sea once you're done.

LOOKING AT PLANTS

Animals are not the only live things that you would see on the seashore. There are plants, too—not corn and beans, of course, but plants that are especially fitted for living in the water. Some are green. Some are blue-green. Some are brown and some are red.

If you lift a stone out of the water you may find plants growing on it. If you look down in the water you may find plants growing from the sandy bottom.

Tides and high waves bring plants to the seashore and make small piles of them. Small seashore animals sometimes stay in piles of seaweed until the tide comes in and carries them out again. When the animals are in these piles of seaweed they can stay moist. You may find small starfish and sea snails and clams and crabs in these heaps of seaweed on the shore. Place some in a pail of seawater and use your magnifying glass to look at the tiny creatures that come out of the weeds. Look at the sea plants, too. You may be surprised at what you see.

If you look carefully at a pile of seaweed you may make some interesting discoveries. Some kinds of seaweed have tiny balloons of air that make the seaweed light, so they float when they are in the water. If you squeeze them they pop.

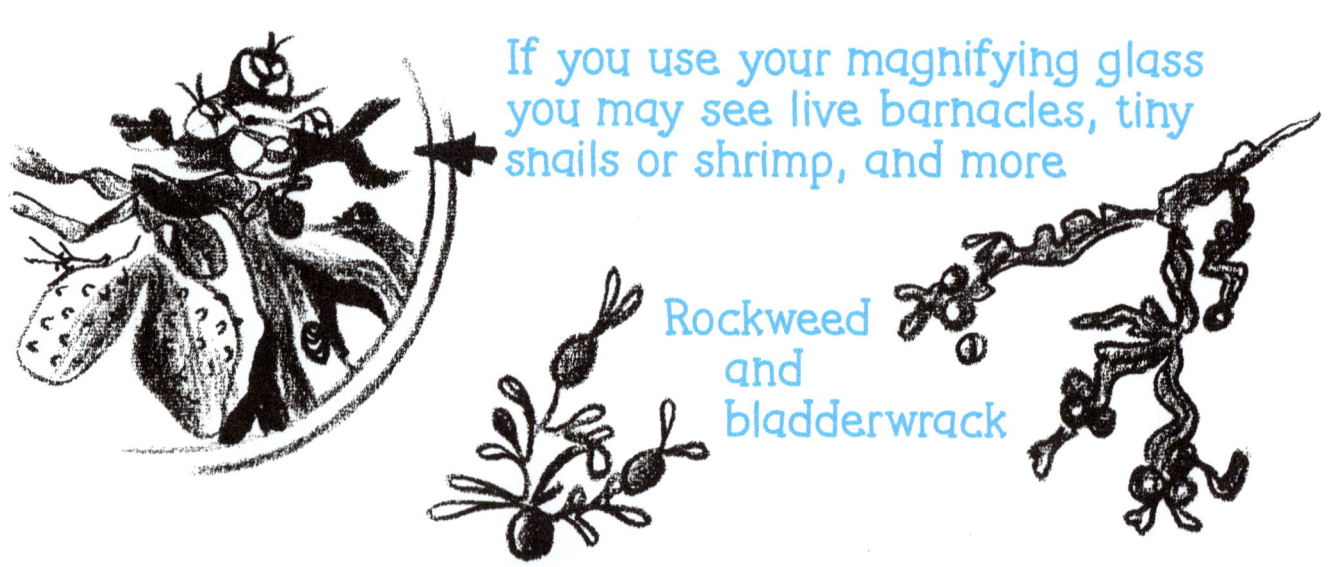

If you use your magnifying glass you may see live barnacles, tiny snails or shrimp, and more

Rockweed and bladderwrack

Sea lettuce

Sea lettuce often gets washed ashore. Its wide leaves are as green as garden lettuce, and it makes fine food for many sea animals. Sea lettuce is large and easy to see, but there are hundreds and hundreds of kinds of sea plants that are so small you need a microscope to see them. These plants float in the seawater, and all kinds of animals eat them. You remember that these plants go into the tubes of clams, they go into the mouths of fish, they settle on rocks, and snails scrape them off with their rough tongues. Water plants are very important to the animals that live in the sea, just as land plants are important to you.

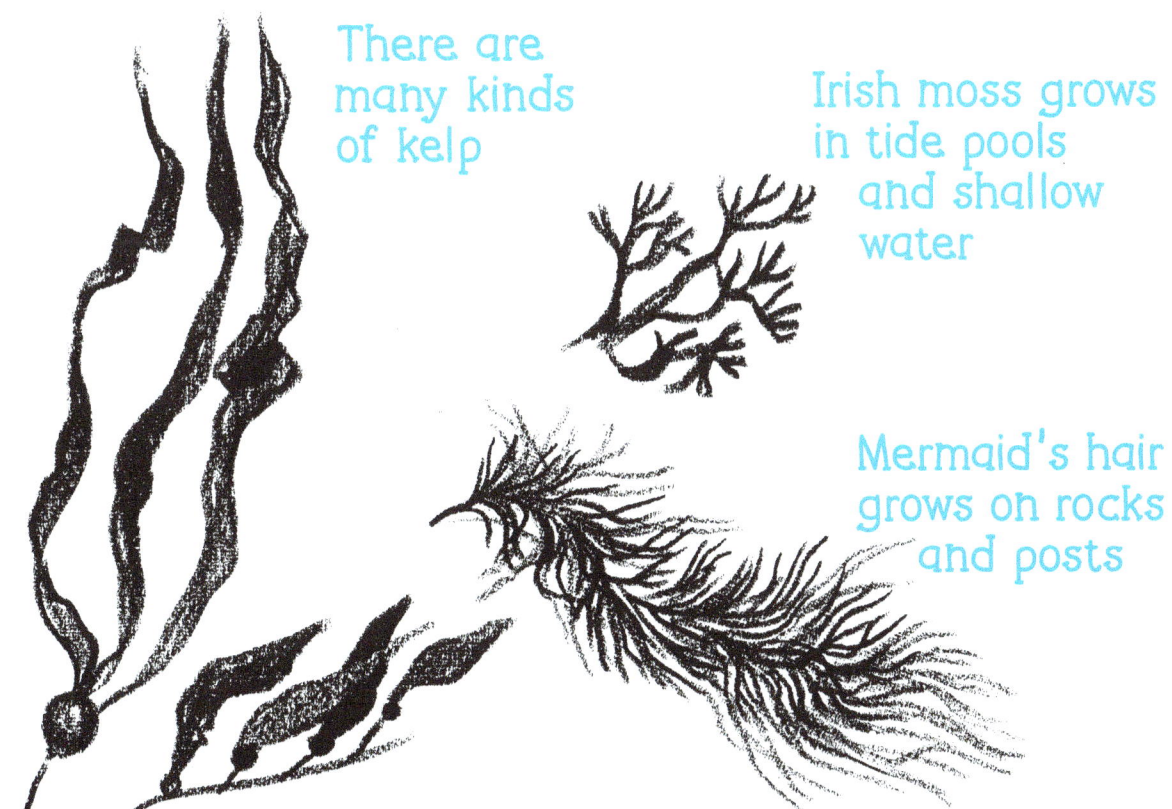

There are many kinds of kelp

Irish moss grows in tide pools and shallow water

Mermaid's hair grows on rocks and posts

LIVING ON THE SEASHORE

The shore of the sea is not the easiest place in the world for animals to live. An animal with a thin skin like a jellyfish dries out very fast if it gets tossed on the shore and the sun shines on it. A dry jellyfish soon dies if it is out of water.

A swimming animal can't walk. If it gets left on the shore when the tide goes out, it can't move about to get food or to get back into the water, and the sun dries it out and it dies.

Animals must have air or they cannot live. Animals that live underwater have gills for getting air. They get the air from the water, but they can't get air on land. So if water animals are left high and dry on land for very long, they die, unless they have special ways to save water between high and low tide.

Animals along the shore eat each other. Gulls eat clams. Snails drill into clams and eat them. Clams eat the tiny sea creatures that come in with the water. So do starfish. So do oysters. Every animal seems to have some enemies, and seashore animals must have ways to protect themselves just as land animals do. Starfish have spiny skin. So do some of their relatives. Clams and snails have hard shells and so do many other seashore animals. Clams dig in the ground, then their enemies can't find them. Some other seashore animals do this. Some live under rocks or in piles of seaweed that the tide sweeps in. Jellyfish sting their enemies. Seashore animals have ways to protect themselves from their enemies, and it's a good thing for them that they do.

These are some of the things you may discover on the shore. Remember to look again and use a magnifying glass so you will see twice as much. Remember to walk slowly and look in all the likely places. Remember that it's no time to skip when you are trying to find out who lives at the seashore. You may whistle if you like. Barnacles and jellyfish won't hear you. Neither will snails and fiddler crabs. Your friend may hear you and come too, and then you can show each other the things you see, and soon you may both know who lives at the seashore.

Published by Purple House Press, purplehousepress.com
Written in 1962 by Glenn Blough. Copyright © 2024 by Purple House Press
ISBN 9781948959858

Discover more captivating books from Glenn Blough and Jeanne Bendick!

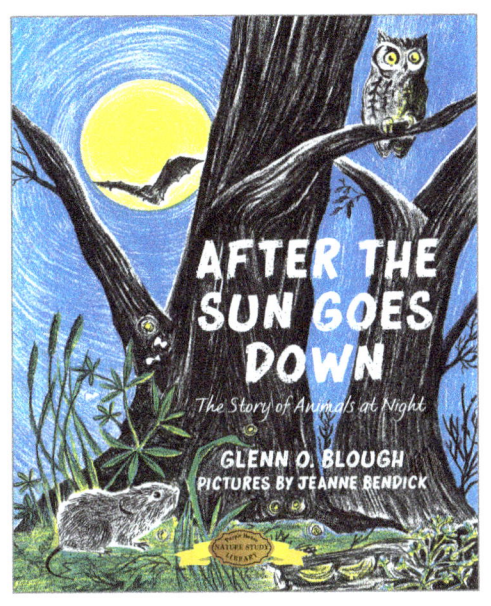

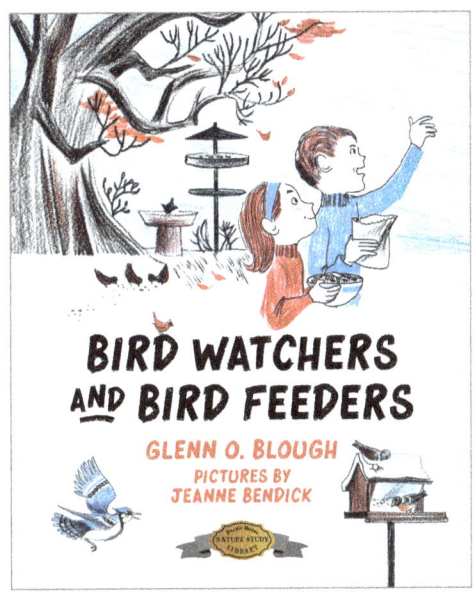